STORIES OF THE PEOPLE

Unku (man's Ollantay [folk drama] theater garment) ca. 1930. Cuzco, Peru. 102 x 57.5 cm. (13.3299)

Stories of the People

Native American Voices

NATIONAL MUSEUM OF THE AMERICAN INDIAN
SMITHSONIAN INSTITUTION
IN ASSOCIATION WITH
UNIVERSE PUBLISHING

Project Director, NMAI: Terence Winch
Editors, NMAI: Holly Stewart and Cheryl Wilson
Photo Editor, NMAI: Lou Stancari
Researcher, NMAI: John McKinn
Editor, Universe: Sandra Gilbert
Designed by Reiner Design, NYC

First published in the United States of America in 1997
by UNIVERSE PUBLISHING
A Division of Rizzoli International Publications, Inc.
300 Park Avenue South
New York, NY 10010

97 98 99 00 01 / 10 9 8 7 6 5 4 3 2 1

Library of Congress Catalog Card Number: 97–60148

Printed in Hong Kong

Published in conjunction with the exhibition *Stories of the People*, on view at the Arts & Industries Building, Smithsonian Institution,
Washington, D.C., 10 August 1996–10 August 1997.

The exhibition *Stories of the People* is made possible through the generosity of the Greenwich Workshop, Inc.

Front cover: *Llclla* (textile manta), 18th c. Peru. 63 x 55 cm. (14.3681)
Back cover: Makah women. Washington State. (N36535)
Endpapers: Lakota tipi cover. South Dakota. Base to apex: 487.7 cm. (20.7813)

CONTENTS

6

Two girls, probably Kiowa,
ca. 1890. (N37975)

FOREWORD

Remembering What We Have Been Told

For Native people, stories are a matter of sustenance, part of the very food of life. In the early 1930s, Her Eyes Grey, a White Mountain Apache, told how, when she was young, a basket of corn was provided during the telling of a long story: "...and for each line that was spoken, that person who was listening would count out one corn seed. This way there would be sometimes two hundred corn seeds. Then that person would have to eat them all. If he could eat them, then he would remember all the words he had been told." In the Native universe, the oral tradition keeps cultural truths alive as surely as food sustains the body.

For *Stories of the People*, we have asked seven Native Americans, each of whom embodies a rich store of cultural insight and authority, to tell us the histories and some of the stories of their people. To help achieve this end, they chose telling works from the collections of the National Museum of the American Indian, some of which are illustrated in this book. I use the adjective "telling" quite deliberately, for Native objects are always interwoven into Native societies in ways that carry complex meaning and significance. These artifacts have a deeply narrative, often spiritual, quality that transcends their purely aesthetic dimension, as I hope you will clearly see in this book. We have also uncovered stories from traditional sources that bring added resonance to the contributors' texts. These stories, of course, are every bit as crucial to their cultures as the historical narratives. As contributor Dale Curtis Miles so aptly expresses, "We do not like our stories referred to as myths; our sense of who we are and our world view are wrapped up in these stories. Even clothing, tools, baskets, and other material culture so important in everyday life have direct links to the stories of the people."

The book and the accompanying exhibition represent the effort and dedication of many people from the staff of the National Museum of the American Indian and of other branches of the Smithsonian Institution. The museum would also like to acknowledge the contributions of individuals and organizations outside the Smithsonian who were instrumental to this project. I particularly wish to thank the seven contributors—Ramiro Matos, Jorge Flores Ochoa, Charlotte Heth, George P. Horse Capture, Dale Curtis Miles, Greig Arnold, and Richard W. Hill, Sr.—for their wonderful words and stories. In addition, I want to express our gratitude for the generous support of the Greenwich Workshop, Inc.

Stories of the People reflects the museum's unique mission and commitment to present Native life and culture through the voices of Native people. The book and exhibition highlight the beauty of Native artistic expression, touch upon personal memories, and represent continuity with the past as it affirms the vitality of contemporary arts and culture in Native life.

—*W. Richard West, Director*
(Southern Cheyenne and member of the
Cheyenne and Arapaho Tribes of Oklahoma)

7

Shooting Star (Sioux).

(P22408)

NORTHERN PLAINS

The Struggle for Land and a Way of Life
George P. Horse Capture (A'ani [Gros Ventre])

An enduring principle of early Plains Indian culture is a view of the world that embraces all things on earth and sees them as siblings. Each of earth's inhabitants deserves respect from all other beings. They must live together in balance, all dependent upon each other.

The one responsible for everything is the One Above, the all-powerful: not a vengeful god, but a Great Spirit. A time-honored Plains Indian manner of worshiping the Great Spirit is through dreams or visions. These holy activities often take place on the tops of buttes or mountains, where individuals go to fast for four days and nights. It was during these dreams or visions that the Plains Indians received tobacco, corn, the horse, the pipe, and all of the other critical gifts needed for survival.

TREATIES AND LAND LOSS

The First Peoples of the Plains and others view themselves as distinct sovereign nations. When two nations made an agreement, both sides may have sworn to respect it on their sacred word, or consecrated it with a special ceremony. When the white men came, they had little respect for the First People's sovereignty. For them, a treaty was a way of claiming territory for white settlers while pushing the tribes onto ever-shrinking lands.

In September 1851, a grand treaty council met near Fort Laramie in the Wyoming Territory. The Teton Sioux came, as did the Cheyenne, Arapaho, Assiniboine, Crow, Gros Ventre, and Arikara—perhaps 10,000 in all. Tribes who had never seen each other off the battlefield were now in one camp. A government spokesman addressed them, saying that the Great White Father had heard his red children's complaints about the destruction of the buffalo and the encroachment of the settlers, and would make restitution. In turn, the Indian people had to allow whites to travel unmolested and to establish forts. If the tribes agreed to this, he said, Indian lands would not be taken away. This was the promise, but gradually the treaty of 1851—and others that followed in 1855, 1868, and later—took our lands, and most everything else, away.

Sioux cradleboard, ca. 1890. Canvas, hide, glass beads, silk ribbons, wood, brass tacks, length 100 cm. (21.1436) *Right*: Eastern Sioux deerhide coat with quilled decoration, ca. 1890. Length 81 cm. (10.4309)

The most prominent features of this shirt are the "American" design elements, foremost among them being the American flag, followed by the eagle and the star.

With the signing of the treaties, the eagles were caged. No more could they freely travel and hunt in their traditional patterns. Food was doled out as a disciplinary device by corrupt agents while the tribes starved.

Facing an end to their way of life, the tribes embarked on a campaign of armed conflicts with the invaders—as other patriots have done. But it was too late. There were now more whites than grass on the prairie, and they kept coming. Out of this desperate time came legends—Chief Joseph, Sitting Bull, Black Kettle, Crazy Horse, Little Raven, and many others—patriots all.

In 1889, Wovoka, a Paiute holy man from Nevada, began to preach a message given to him in a dream. He said that if the people sang certain songs, danced in a certain style, prayed, and treated their neighbors well in the Indian way, then three things would happen: dead ancestors would return, the buffalo would return, and, most important of all, the white man would go away. Wovoka's message spread quickly and

DREAM OF THE CROW AND OWL

The story excerpted here begins, "No man can succeed in life alone, and he cannot get the help he wants from men; therefore he seeks help through some bird or animal which Wakan'tanka sends for his assistance." As a young man, Śiya'ka wished to have a dream that would tell him what his guardian animals would be. Following the instructions of a medicine man, he carried buffalo robes and tobacco to a hilltop, set them out as offerings to the four directions, and awaited his dream. A lifetime later, he called the dream his most cherished possession.

All night I stood with my eyes closed. Just before daybreak I saw a bright light coming toward me from the east. It was a man. His head was tied up, and he held a tomahawk in his hand. He said, "Follow me," and in an instant he changed into a crow. In my dream I followed the crow to a village. He entered the largest tent. When he entered the tent he changed to a man again. Opposite the entrance sat a young man, painted red, who welcomed me. When I was thus received I felt highly honored, for as this was the largest tent I knew it must be the tent of the chief. The young man said he was pleased to see me there. He said, further, that all the animals and birds were his friends, and that he wished me to follow the way that he had used to secure their friendship. He told me to lift my head. I did this and saw dragonflies, butterflies, and all kinds of small insects, while above them flew all kinds of birds. As soon as I cast down my eyes again and looked at the young man and at the man who had brought me thither, I saw that the young man had become transformed into an owl, and that my escort had changed again into a crow.

The owl said, "Always look toward the west when you make a petition, and you will have a long life." After this the owl commanded me to look at him. As soon as I did this he was changed to an elk, and at his feet were the elk medicine and a hoop. As soon as I saw him changing, I began to wonder what marvel would be next. Then I heard a song. I tried to learn the song, and before I realized what I was doing, I was singing the song.

I was a young man at that time and eager to go on the warpath and make a name for myself. After this dream, my stronghold was in the east, but the west was also a source from which I could get help. All the birds and insects I had seen in my dream were things on which I knew I should keep my mind and learn their ways. When the season returns, the birds and insects return with the same colorings as the previous year. They are not all on the earth, but are above it. My mind must be the same. The elk is brave, always helping the women, and in that way the elk has saved a large portion of his tribe. In this I should follow the elk, remembering that the elk, the birds, and the insects are my helpers. I never killed an elk nor ate its flesh. The birds that continually fly in the air I would not kill. I may kill water birds and grass birds if suitable for food, but only these.

—Śiya'ka (Yankton Nakota), 1912

Above: A'ani (Gros Ventre)
tobacco bag, ca. 1880.
Deerhide, porcupine quills,
87.5 x 16.25 cm. (4.2437)
Opposite: Spies on the Enemy
(Absaroke [Crow]), ca. 1898.
Photo by F.A. Rinehart.
(N36494)

became a movement called the Ghost Dance. When the Ghost Dance arrived in the Northern Plains, local officials were alarmed to see the Sioux uniting once again. It all ended on December 29, 1890, at Wounded Knee, a Sioux settlement in South Dakota. The U.S. Army surrounded a group of Sioux Indians and tried to disarm them. A gun was fired. When the screaming stopped, nearly four hundred Sioux lay dead, primarily women and children, slaughtered under a flag of truce. Eighteen U.S. soldiers received Congressional Medals of Honor for what they did that day.

The American way of life has not been too good for American Indian people. Yet we have great respect for the flag. Perhaps this is because Indians have a strong warrior tradition, and when the buffalo days ended, this warrior tradition continued. Today we still honor our warriors—the veterans who served with the U.S. military—and one symbol of that honor is the American flag. Then, too, we respect that flag because it represents our mountains, prairies, rivers, the land where we have always been.

OUR "FIFTY-FIVE"

When I was a child on the Fort Belknap Reservation in Montana, my family lived in great poverty, but we didn't know we were poor. Everybody lived that way on our reservation. On occasion, when all we had to eat were potatoes, my grandmother would say: "We must wait for the better times. When we get our 'fifty-five,' we will have money to throw at the birds."

Later, I learned what my grandmother had meant. Our tribe never received full payment for the treaty we signed in 1855. Indian people signed that treaty—they gave up their land—and all through the years their descendants were always waiting for the government to do its part. Many years later, we did get a small payment for that treaty, but by then my grandmother had passed on to the other side.

Encampment of Bloods,
Piegans, and Sarsi. Near
Gleichen, Alberta, Canada.
(N41393)

In order to express and
validate their heroic
deeds, warriors
recorded these exploits
for public view on
clothing, tipis, and robes.
Here a Blackfeet warrior
depicted his exploits on
his wife's dress.
The deeds include
numerous skirmishes,
including one with a
non-Indian. This brave
warrior survived
several gunshots.

16

Blackfeet muslin dress with
painted decoration, ca. 1900.
Length 126.25 cm. (17.6078)

Above: Absaroke (Crow) male doll, ca. 1915. Deerhide, glass beads, wool cloth, hair, length 31.25 cm. (22.4814) *Right:* Ute bandolier bag, ca. 1855. Deerhide, red wool cloth, seed beads, 67.5 x 45 cm. (8.498)

SURVIVAL

The reservation borders that kept the First Peoples inside also kept others out. A reservation is both a prison and a sanctuary, filled with pride and love for one's own. This Indian land that came from treaties keeps us Indian and always will.

Onslaughts against Indian country have not ceased. Farmers still want Indian water, timber companies want the trees, ranchers want the grass, and mining companies strip our mountains for gold. Today warriors show their strength by protecting their families and traditions until life improves; leaders now must prove themselves by taking action to preserve their people, way of life, and remaining resources.

Today many reservations have junior colleges with ever-growing numbers of students, for we realize that education is key to our survival. Tribal members are earning college degrees as never before. Others are taking up the ways of their ancestors and reviving traditional belief systems and philosophies. The tribes are adapting.

As long as there are children, the people will survive.

18

Absaroke (Crow) Lodge Grass
War Dancers, *from left*: Edward
Wolf Lays Down, Leo Bad
Horse, and Bird Far Away.
Crow Agency, Montana.
(N31485)

"They brought us here to a windy country, and we supposed the wind had blown the goods away; but we heard afterwards that there were some found in the houses in the stockade. We heard that the agent traded some of our goods away, and we suppose he traded them for robes and furs. We think if he had not traded them away there would have been plenty to go round, and the women would not have been crying with cold."

—*Passing Hail (Santee Dakota), 1865*

TUSCARORA

Keeping the Circle of Tradition Strong

Richard W. Hill, Sr. (Tuscarora)

We call our nation Ska Roo Reh. Wars with English colonists, Catawbas, Cherokees, and others forced us to leave North Carolina in search of peace. Seeking the protection of our northern brothers, the Tuscarora became the Sixth Nation of the Great Iroquois Confederacy of Peace in the 1720s. We settled in western New York, the last of our many homeplaces, on land ceded by the Holland Land Company and the Seneca Nation. Together, the Seneca, Cayuga, Onondaga, Oneida, Mohawk, and Tuscarora Nations are called Iroquois, but we prefer the name Haudenosaunee, meaning People of the Long House, a metaphor for our living together in peace under one common law.

An 1845 census gives us a glimpse into Tuscarora life 150 years ago. The family names are still the same—Jacobs, Mount Pleasant, Chew, Hewitt, Johnson, Printup, Pembleton, Green, Gansworth, Patterson, Smith, Cusick, Fish, Henry—but much has changed. In 1845, 322 people lived on the Tuscarora Reservation; in 1996, about 1,200 people. In 1845, there were 60 farmers; in 1996, only about a dozen large-scale farmers. In 1845, 247 Tuscarora practiced the Native religion and 63 practiced Christianity; in 1996, there are fewer than 50 traditional Tuscarora, and the Baptist Church is the dominant spiritual force. One hundred and fifty years ago nearly everyone on the reservation spoke fluent Tuscarora; today only a few speakers remain.

Yet four traditions have helped our people retain their unique cultural identity: farming, beadwork, lacrosse, and the Council of Chiefs.

Seneca lacrosse players, ca. 1910. Cattaraugus Reservation, New York. Photo by Alanson B. Skinner. (N1701)

FARMING: CONNECTION TO THE LAND

Three principal crops, called the Three Sisters—*oo-nhae-hah* (corn), *oo-thaw-hah-rah* (beans), and *kawj-hah-whath* (squash)—have been the primary foods of the Tuscarora in both North Carolina and New York. Our farming traditions helped to re-establish the nation after we settled in New York in the 1700s, and again after the War of 1812, when British troops burned nearly every Tuscarora home and farm.

Farming traditions set an annual rhythm to life at Tuscarora. The Tuscarora ceremonial cycle follows the seasons. As crops ripen, we offer rituals of thanksgiving. Every New Year's Day, a community feast is held to thank the Creator for all He has provided, and to celebrate the beginning of a new cycle of life. To us, the land and crops are sacred gifts.

LACROSSE: A MEANINGFUL GAME FOR MEN

We call the game *yoo-nhae'-rhoo-haws*. The French renamed it lacrosse. It has its roots in the dawn of the Iroquoian universe. At the time of Creation, twin boys were born on the newly created Turtle Island. They were great rivals and fought continuously for dominance over the new land, playing lacrosse to a draw. Lacrosse became the Creator's favorite game.

Opposite: The Hill family marks rows for corn-planting, 1941. Photo by Alma Hill (© Alma Hill), courtesy Richard W. Hill, Sr. *Above:* Tuscarora wooden spoon. Length 24 cm. (22.7648)

For countless years, the Tuscarora have played lacrosse against the Seneca, Onondaga, Oneida, Cayuga, and Mohawk. The old games were great contests of skill, speed, and endurance, with hundreds of players on wide open fields. In 1880 the National Lacrosse Association of Canada banned Indians from championship play. A century later, the Haudenosaunee formed their own national team, which includes Tuscarora players. The team now competes in international championships, traveling overseas on Iroquois passports, under an Iroquois flag.

BEADWORK: A MEANINGFUL ROLE FOR WOMEN

By the mid 1800s, when times were hard, beadwork became a way to supplement family income. Tuscarora women who sold their work to tourists were cultural mediators, using beadwork to balance the changing social, religious, and economic forces in their community.

Tuscarora embossed beadwork is distinctive, influenced by Native symbolism and Victorian taste. It features overlapping rows of beads in graduated colors that create a raised effect. This style of beadwork has also helped the Tuscarora keep a sense of identity, recalling ancient patterns of decoration and symbolic imagery.

A young girl and her elderly mother lived in a large village along the shores of the upper Niagara River. The girl was very sickly and could not attract the attentions of any young man, and she and her mother lived alone for many years. One day, the mother went off to visit another village, and told her daughter that she would be gone quite some time. The mother told her daughter to keep the door locked shut until she returned, and the girl dutifully agreed.

Late that night, someone knocked on the door of the girl's longhouse. "What do you want?" she asked. "I want you to open the door for me. I want to be with you," came the reply from beyond the door. The voice was nice and gentle so the girl opened the door despite what her mother had told her. In walked the most handsome man she had ever seen. He seemed to be very pleasant and well behaved.

The visitor told the girl he wanted to marry her, and she was so excited by his attention that they slept together. She noticed he wore a beautiful necklace made of white clam shells that shone like silver. The shells were small in the front and grew larger where the necklace ended at his shoulders. The two stayed together several days, but one morning the man said he had to return to his home. He took one of the large shells from his shoulder and said, "This will serve to remind you of me while I am gone."

"Will you not be coming back?" asked the girl. He shook his head no. She was devastated by the shocking news that he was leaving her. He tried to make her feel better by saying, "Some day I will return to you," but he did not really mean it.

The next morning, the girl's mother returned, and it did not take her long to realize that someone else had been in her home. She became suspicious and asked her daughter if anyone had come to visit. The girl told her mother the truth about what had happened. She pulled out the clam shell that the visitor had given her, explaining that the man was the most handsome she had ever seen. In looking at the bright shell, they realized that what looked like a shell was actually a large scale, like that of a fish or snake.

The mother began to cry, knowing what had happened. "It was not a man that you were with," she told her shocked daughter. "It was a giant snake who took advantage of you because you are ill."

It was not long before the girl discovered she was pregnant. As her stomach grew larger, she became sleepier and sleepier. Finally she became so large that all she could do was lie down in the sunshine and sleep all day long. One day her mother came upon her sleeping in some brush and was

I learned early in life that Niagara Falls held a different meaning for me than for the many tourists I saw there. They were often told the story of the "Maid of the Mist," in which a young woman is sacrificed over the falls by local Indians. Even as a young boy, I knew this story was untrue, but I didn't hear the Tuscarora story of another girl's experience at the falls until I was an adult. This version, recorded by my great-grandfather's brother, J.N.B. Hewitt, reflects a reverence for the power of the falls and the spirits who reside there that are an integral part of Tuscarora history.

astonished to see a mass of tiny, entangled snakes magically appear next to the girl. When the snakes saw her, they retreated back into the body of her sleeping daughter. She knew these snakes were powerful spirits.

The old woman had to tell her daughter that her belly was full of snakes. This news terrified the girl and she ran off into the woods to try to escape the truth. She ran to the Niagara River above the great waterfall and threw herself into the water. The girl swiftly floated toward the brink of the falls, and as she drifted over the cascade to what she thought would be certain death, a strange thing happened: the Thunderbeings, who lived in caves behind the great falls, reached out and caught the girl, saving her from the crushing power of the falls. There were four Thunderbeings—three young ones, and one very old elder Thunderbeing. They told her that they knew what was bothering her, and led her to their lodge, where the oldest one began to make medicine to cure the girl of her unwanted pregnancy.

The medicine worked, and a jumble of snakes began to fall out of the girl's stomach. The elder Thunderbeing told her not to fear, for the snakes were a fine food. The Thunderbeings grabbed up and cooked them, enjoying a great feast as they ate every last one of the snakes. Then they turned their attention back to the girl and gave her more medicine, as she had grown weak.

Slowly the girl recovered and she lived with the Thunderbeings. One day, she met another Thunderbeing and they quickly fell in love. Again the girl became pregnant, but this time, the elder Thunderbeing explained that she must return to her mother, so that she could be cared for properly. The girl's Thunderbeing lover could not stay with her, but had to return to the lodge behind the falls. He told her that she would have a baby boy, and that she must not let him play with other children. If the boy ever got mad at others, he could make lightning, and that would be very dangerous. Further, the Thunderbeing told her that when the boy grew older, he must be kept indoors when the other Thunderbeings called out to him, or else he would disappear with them.

After the girl gave birth to her son, she dutifully locked the little boy in the longhouse whenever thunder rolled across the sky. But he cried relentlessly to go outside. This continued for many years until he became a young man. One day his mother went visiting and forgot to lock him in the house. He waited until she disappeared into the woods and then bolted through the open door. As he stepped out-doors, the Thunderers spoke to him from the sky above. He walked towards them and their voices got louder. Then the son, born of the love of the sickly girl and the Thunderbeing, vanished into the sky to join his father's relatives.

THE COUNCIL OF CHIEFS

The Tuscarora Nation still operates under its traditional form of government. It is organized around several extended families, or clans—Turtle, Bear, Wolf, Beaver, Snipe, Eel, and Deer—whose members are related through female ancestry. Each clan is headed by a Clan Mother, usually the eldest woman, who selects the male leader—a Chief—subject to the approval of her clan. The Chiefs of each clan meet to deliberate on issues and decide how to deal with them. They also represent the Tuscarora Nation in the Grand Council of the Iroquois Confederacy, meeting with Chiefs of the Seneca, Cayuga, Onondaga, Oneida, and Mohawk nations.

The Chief must be honest, kind-hearted, and able to withstand criticism. He must not have committed any crimes, nor ever have left his family. He should have a good knowledge of the laws and traditions of the Iroquois Confederacy, represent his people fairly, and always be concerned for their welfare. A man becomes Chief once he has been accepted by the Council of Chiefs. All Chiefs have equal authority; there is no head Chief. A Chief can be removed from office if the Clan Mother feels that he no longer has the people's welfare at heart.

The Chiefs are the first and last line of defense for the sovereignty of the nation. During the past 150 years, both federal and state governments have challenged Indian sovereignty over land, jurisdiction, citizenship, the military draft, taxation, and education. Recently, a "warrior society" and a business council tried to overthrow the Council of Chiefs and bring high-stakes gambling to the Tuscarora Reservation. During this struggle over our future, most people remained committed to the Council of Chiefs, which represents the integrity of the nation, the continuity of our traditions, and our hope for the future.

Ge-Keah-Saw-Sa (Caroline Parker), a member of the Wolf Clan and relative of Gen. Ely S. Parker (Seneca), ca. 1870. New York. (34330)

Cherokee players lined up for the ball game, 1908. (N26853)

CHEROKEE

Surviving the Trail of Tears

Charlotte Heth (Cherokee)

We call ourselves Aniyunwiya, the real people. Our story is one of balance—men and women, animals and plants, complementing one another's lives. It is also one of changes, upsets of balance, relocation, adaptation, and survival into the twenty-first century.

The Cherokees were the original hunters, mountaineers, and Piedmont farmers of the southeastern United States, inhabiting parts of what are now seven states. Starting with the creation of the first man and woman, men became hunters, and women, farmers; men also helped clear the fields and plant the crops, while women helped process the meat and hides from hunting. Both farming and hunting were essential to the Cherokee way of life. Fishing was a family activity, with men doing the heavy work and women making the fish traps and fish baskets. Although basketweaving was women's work, men helped gather and process the raw materials for these and other baskets.

Growing up Cherokee, as well as American, meant living in towns or settlements of cabins along forested river valleys. Because Cherokees trace their ancestry through their mothers and grandmothers, several generations of a family used to live together in the women's houses. Usually the women planted small gardens near the house, but most of the family's vegetables were grown in large, communal fields.

Men made all the wooden implements. Women made and used baskets, and pottery vessels with designs that were either stamped with paddles or cut into the wet clay. Cherokee women have been making baskets continuously from the earliest times up to today, to store all kinds of items, to use in preparing and gathering food, to give as gifts, and to sell. Even today in North Carolina, some families keep baskets that have been handed down in their families for more than 150 years. Men and women work together to harvest and process the basketry materials— cane, white oak, honeysuckle, hickory bark, and various dyeing and decorating materials. Cherokee women still hand-coil pots, which are fired using charcoal, corncobs, bark, and corn for fuel.

THE TRAIL OF TEARS

Our way of life required large tracts of land for trapping, fishing, hunting, and farming; for rituals that called for the use of wild plants and animals, streams of clear running water, and particular landmarks; and for a civilization that needed different kinds of towns—towns of peace and refuge, war and strategy, and ceremony. The British and later the Americans looked at the map and thought that the Cherokees were using only part of their homeland. For three hundred years, soldiers, settlers, missionaries, prospectors, adventurers, travelers, and runaway slaves coveted the Cherokee lands, until, in 1783, the politicians started to seize the "surplus."

When the 1803 Louisiana Purchase opened lands west of the Mississippi, Thomas Jefferson suggested that the Eastern Indians move west. Between 1808 and 1810 a few Cherokees did migrate to Arkansas. Later, in 1828, after Georgia prospectors learned that gold had been found at Dahlonega (the Cherokee word for yellow or gold), the Georgians began persecuting the Cherokees more heavily. But it was Andrew Jackson who actually seized the land for non-Cherokees through the 1835 Treaty of New Echota, forcing Cherokee removal to the West.

Although the majority of the Cherokee Nation refused to sign the treaty, and despite U.S. Supreme Court rulings in the Cherokees' favor, in 1838 and 1839 the U.S. War Department forced the vast majority of the Cherokees, including my ancestors, to move from the Southeast to Indian Territory, now Oklahoma, on the infamous Trail of Tears. Soldiers separated them from family members and possessions, put them in stockades, and guarded them day and night. On foot, the prisoners—men, women, and children—made the 850-mile journey west. Of the 17,000 Cherokees

Opposite left: Cherokee cane and wood "rib" *taluja* (basket), and detail, 1908. Cherokee, North Carolina. Width 22 cm. (1.9163) *Opposite right:* Cherokee cane storage *taluja* (basket) with lid, 1908. Cherokee, North Carolina. Width 54 cm. *(1.9196) Above left:* Cherokee cane and wood "trophy" *taluja* (basket), 1982. Width 33 cm. (25.1333) *Above right:* Cherokee cane food storage *taluja* (basket), 20th c. Cherokee, North Carolina. Height 61.5 cm. (24.6886)

in the 1835 census, between 4,000 and 8,000 died during the Trail of Tears and in the year following—one-third of the Cherokee Nation fell to deprivation, disease, and despair.

RENEWAL: CHEROKEE LANGUAGE, EDUCATION, AND SURVIVAL

In 1821 Sequoyah, a Cherokee, devised a writing system for the Cherokee language. Often called the Cherokee Alphabet, it consists of eighty-six characters, each representing a syllable. In 1828 the *Cherokee Phoenix*, printed in Cherokee and English, became the first Indian newspaper in North America. Newspapers, hymnals, Bibles, and other writings are printed in Cherokee to this day. Handwritten correspondence, diaries, books of Cherokee spiritual knowledge, and accounts of traditional Cherokee organizations survive and are treasured.

The new Cherokee Nation committed itself to education, and in 1841 it appointed a superintendent of education and created eleven public schools. Two institutions of higher learning, the male and female seminaries, opened large permanent buildings in 1851. By 1895 the Cherokee Nation supported not only the two seminaries, but also an orphan asylum that boarded 150 children, and more than one hundred primary schools, educating 48,000 students. Fourteen primary schools were set aside for Negro citizens of the Cherokee Nation, along with a fine high school, supported by the Cherokee government. In addition, there were twelve mission schools.

Eastern Cherokee woman gathering corn, 1908. North Carolina. Photo by M. R. Harrington. (N2736)

In 1889 the U.S. Bureau of American Ethnology received an unsolicited manuscript from Vinita, Indian territory, with a letter saying, "Please examine and if of value to you, remit what you consider an equivalent," signed by Wahnenauhi. The bureau sent the author ten dollars. In later correspondence, she explained, "The name, 'Wahnenauhi,' signed to the Manuscript, is my own Cherokee name. You are at liberty to use either Cherokee, or English name in connection with the Manuscript." Wahnenauhi's manuscript was published in 1966. Here, she describes a scene from the Removal.

[P]erish or remove! it might be,——remove *and* perish! [A] long journey through the Wilderness,——could the little ones endure? [A]nd how about the sick? [T]he old people and infirm, could they possibly endure the long tedious journey; Should they leave?

This had been the home of their Ancestors from time out of mind.

Every thing they held dear on earth was here, *must* they leave?

The graves of their kindred forsaken would be desecrated by the hand of the White Man. The very air seemed filled with an undercurrent of inexpressible sadness and regret....

Some of the Cherokees, remained in their homes, and determined not to leave.

For these soldiers were sent, by Gorgia [sic], and they were gathered up and driven, at the point of the bayonet, into camp with the others. [T]hey were not allowed to take any of their household stuff, but were compelled to leave as they were, with only the clothes which they had on. One old, very old man, asked the soldiers to allow him time to pray once more, with his family in the dear old home, before he left it forever. The answer was, with a brutal oath, "No! no time for prayers. Go!" at the same time giving him a rude push toward the door.

In many instances, the families of settlers were at hand, and as the Indians were evicted, the whites entered, taking full possession of every thing left.

——Wahnenauhi (Cherokee), 1889

35

Above: Cherokee blowgun darts. Cane and locust wood. (24.8845B-D) *Right:* Cherokee man with blowgun and darts, child with doll, 1928. Cherokee, North Carolina. Photo by Bob Becker. *Opposite:* Cherokee child's hide moccasins, 1908. Cherokee, North Carolina. Length 13 cm. (1.9054)

Eventually, political and economic pressures in both Oklahoma and North Carolina forced the Cherokees to occupy smaller and smaller tracts of land and to seek wage labor. In the early 1900s, tourists and collectors began buying North Carolina Cherokee baskets, pottery, and other crafts. Although Cherokee men took day-labor jobs to raise cash, they also made and sold a few wooden items and blow-guns. Women, however, consistently earned money from making baskets, often traveling long distances on foot to sell them. Many of the decorative, novelty baskets are made primarily for sale to non-Cherokees.

Before Europeans arrived, we were 30,000 in number; by 1700, the Cherokee population was 16,000. Today, more than 200,000 people identify themselves as Cherokee, East and West, although not all are enrolled members of the federally rec-ognized tribes, and many are mixed-bloods. A majority still live in Oklahoma or in North Carolina, where industry, agriculture, and tourism drive the economy. Cherokees today visit back and forth, covering the long distance by car or plane. To maintain or restore balance or harmony in their lives, Cherokees will go to great lengths. In the face of challenges, the Cherokee people persevere through adaptation and continuation of language and customs.

"In History, little is said of this event, so laden with loss and suffering to the Cherokee Indians.... It is only what has been repeated many times since, in the case of other Indian tribes.... Gold had been found in some parts of the Nation, and this fact, by exciting the cupidity of the Whites, had brought to a crisis the circumstances which resulted in the removal."

—*Wahnenauhi (Cherokee), 1889*

INDIAN WOMAN POUNDING CORN
CHEROKEE RESERVATION, N.C

I-P-14

The Pheasant once saw a woman beating corn in a wooden mortar in front of the house. "I can do that too," he said, but the woman would not believe it, so the Pheasant went into the woods and got upon a hollow log and drummed with his wings as a pheasant does, until the people in the house heard him and thought he was really beating corn.

—*Ităgû'nǎhǐ (Cherokee), ca. 1888*

39

Cherokee woman pounding corn, ca. 1931. Cherokee, North Carolina. (P15130)

Once the animals challenged the birds to a great ballplay, and the birds accepted. The leaders made the arrangements and fixed the day, and when the time came both parties met at the place for the ball dance, the animals on a smooth grassy bottom near the river and the birds in the treetops over by the ridge. The captain of the animals was the Bear, who was so strong and heavy that he could pull down anyone who got in his way. All along the road to the ball ground he was tossing up great logs to show his strength and boasting of what he would do to the birds when the game began. The Terrapin, too—not the little one we have now, but the great original Terrapin—was with the animals. His shell was so hard that the heaviest blows could not hurt him, and he kept rising up on his hind legs and dropping heavily again to the ground, bragging that this was the way he would crush any bird that tried to take the ball from him. Then there was the Deer, who could outrun every other animal. Altogether it was a fine company.

The birds had the Eagle for their captain, with the Hawk and the great Tlă'nuwă, all swift and strong of flight, but still they were a little afraid of the animals. The dance was over and they were all pruning their feathers up in the trees and waiting for the captain to give the word when here came two little things hardly larger than field mice climbing up the tree in which sat perched the bird captain. At last they reached the top, and creeping along the limb to where the Eagle captain sat they asked to be allowed to join in the game. The captain looked at them, and seeing that they were four-footed, he asked why they did not go to the animals, where they belonged. The little things said that they had, but the animals had made fun of them and driven them off because they were so small. Then the bird captain pitied them and wanted to take them.

But how could they join the birds when they had no wings? The Eagle, the Hawk, and the others consulted, and at last it was decided to make some wings for the little

Cherokee dances, songs, and games serve both ceremony and pleasure. Although the stickball game appears to be recreational, it is traditionally preceded by a complex set of activities that include fasting, medicine, ritual bathing, and songs and dances by men and women. In the past, the game was played to settle disputes between towns or clans. Then and now, men play the water drum and hand-held rattles while women wear the terrapin-shell leg rattles to set the beat for the dances. Often a feast follows.

This story of a ball game between the birds and animals is told by Cherokees in North Carolina and Oklahoma. Tlă'nuwă, one of the birds' leaders, is a great hawk.

fellows. They tried for a long time to think of something that might do, until someone happened to remember the drum they had used in the dance. The head was of groundhog skin and maybe they could cut off a corner and make wings out of it. So they took two pieces of leather from the drumhead and cut them into shape for wings and stretched them with cane splints and fastened them on to the forelegs of one of the small animals, and in this way came Tla'mehă, the Bat. They threw the ball to him and told him to catch it, and by the way he dodged and circled about, keeping the ball always in the air and never letting it fall to the ground, the birds soon saw that he would be one of their best men.

Now they wanted to fix the other little animal, but they had used up all their leather to make wings for the Bat, and there was no time to send for more. Somebody said they might do it by stretching his skin, so two large birds took hold from opposite sides with their strong bills, and by pulling at his fur for several minutes they managed to stretch the skin on each side between the fore and hind feet, until they had Tewa, the Flying Squirrel. To try him the bird captain threw up the ball, and the Flying Squirrel sprang off the limb after it, caught it in his teeth, and carried it through the air to another tree nearly across the bottom.

When they were all ready the signal was given and the game began, but almost at the first toss the Flying Squirrel caught the ball and carried it up a tree, from which he threw it to the birds, who kept it in the air for some time until it dropped. The Bear rushed to get it, but the Martin darted after it and threw it to the Bat, who was flying near the ground, and by his dodging and doubling kept it out of the way of even the Deer, until he finally threw it between the posts and won the game for the birds.

The Bear and the Terrapin, who had boasted so of what they would do, never got a chance even to touch the ball. For saving the ball when it dropped, the birds afterwards gave the Martin a gourd in which to build his nest, and he still has it.

MAKAH

Living in Harmony

Greig Arnold (Makah)

In our language our name is qʷidiccaʔatx (pronounced kwadich cha'ak), which means People Who Live Among the Rocks and Seagulls. It describes our home next to the Pacific Ocean and the Strait of Juan de Fuca. Our stories say that we have lived here since the beginning of time. We have always been whale hunters and fishermen, famed for our skill, which we owe to the wealth of knowledge that our ancestors have given us.

Before contact with non-Indians, our people lived in five villages in what is now Washington State. Biheda and Deah face the Strait of Juan de Fuca; Why-atch, Tsoo-yess, and Ozette look out on the Pacific Ocean. We have occupied these villages for more than four thousand years.

Radical change came when the House on the Water People—Europeans in big ships—sailed into our waters. In 1792 the Spanish claimed our land, but our warriors drove the invaders away. Soon new outsiders were trying to control our property. In 1855 the governor of the Washington Territory signed the Treaty of Neah Bay with us. Our language was not the primary means of negotiation, and we found ourselves renamed Makah, a word from the language of the tribe to the east.

So began the efforts to change us. In spite of our maritime talents and resources, Indian agents and the War Department tried to make us farmers. They tried to eradicate our language and our ceremonies. They sought to displace our elders from their role as teachers. We are still working to retain rights guaranteed to us in our treaty, and to regain the ability to exercise these rights.

Makah woman, ca. 1915.
Photo by Edward S. Curtis.
(P4518)

Makah harpoon barbs with property marks, late 19th/early 20th c. Neah Bay, Washington. Bone, string, height 13.7 cm. (larger of two). (5.9961A-B)

SEA, BEACHES, AND FORESTS

Our ancestors have given us thousands of years of knowledge about the ocean, rivers, lakes, beaches, and forests, and their resources. Our ability to feed ourselves and our guests has been renowned through time. Today, great-grandmothers teach their skills to our children, who learn that their table is set when the tide goes out. We still collect a large variety of shellfish and gather many berries, medicines, and plant foods. Our hunters still provide elk, deer, and bear for winter tables.

The forest provides places for our ceremonies and gives us foods, medicines, and raw materials. The western red cedar gives us houses, canoes, clothing, and containers. It diapers us at birth and shrouds us in death.

Deer and the Canary Bird Dancers

It happened one day that Deer was getting ready to burn the splinters from the bottom of his canoe. He had the strips of cedar ready and the canoe in position. Then a company of women planned to dance and distract his mind. They believed that if they danced long enough he would forget his work, hold the torch too long in one place, and let his canoe burn. They believed this because he had so much curiosity, which, of course, is a characteristic of the animal today.

Deer's wife heard of this and went to him and told him the whole story. He said, "Why should I watch dancers when I am fixing my canoe? I am busy." His wife warned him, saying, "You always forget your work, you are so curious."

The dancers came, and Deer was quite brave for a long time. Then he turned slowly, held his torch too long in one place, and his canoe burned up. His wife said, "I told you you would forget what you were doing."

The dancers were the canary bird girls—*who'whoĭk*—and in their hands they held rattles made of sea-parrot beaks which they shook as they danced. The words of their song were as follows:

Watch, the canary bird girls are dancing.

—*Mrs. Wilson Parker (Makah), 1920s*

"You, Born to Be Given,…go, go and tell your father, your mother, your uncle, your aunt, your elder brothers, and your youngest brothers that you had good luck because you came to this, my fishing canoe."

— *Prayer addressed to a caught fish*

Opposite: Makah man in a dugout canoe, late 19th c. (P10383) *Right:* Model of a Makah canoe, ca. 1900, attributed to Young Doctor, Neah Bay, Washington. Wood, cedar bark, bearskin, and paint, 420 x 90 cm. (6.8874)

TEACHING AND LEARNING

Our children rely on the wisdom of the elders to make life's passages easier. For countless generations they have taught our young people through ceremonies and practical experiences. Elders are responsible for passing on the collective and personal knowledge that our people have accumulated through thousands of years.

We also have many games that teach self-respect, cooperation, observational skills, and leadership. The skills we learn when we play games help prepare us to provide for our families. The cooperation we learn helps us work together to move large canoes, build houses, preserve food for the winter, and hunt whales.

During the winter months in Neah Bay, when the rain never stops and the wind roars over us, the wolves come out to help us move through life. The wolves were the first beings to share their dance with our people. Elders make sure that we remember this gift, and that we use it when we pass from one life stage to another.

Winter is also the proper time for *u.k a.li.*, when novices are initiated into a society that unites the people of our five villages. In learning respect for all living things, novices learn to perform the dances of certain animals and supernatural beings. To wear a headdress and dance the songs of your family takes you to another place and time.

Our dances and societies were targets of the Indian agents who tried to force us to give them up. To preserve our traditions, we observed them on offshore islands and

Above: Makah gambling toggles, 19th c. Neah Bay, Washington. Bone, leather, height 7.3 cm. (larger of the two). (1.9280) *Opposite:* Makah battledores and shuttlecocks, early 20th c. Neah Bay, Washington. Paddle: red cedar, 30.5 x 22.5 cm.; shuttlecocks: wood, feathers, length 15.3 cm. (1.9278A-C)

in other isolated spots. The agents did not prevail. Our elders still teach the traditions, and our songs and dances continue.

OUR SONGS AND DANCES CONTINUE

In the 142 years since we signed our treaty, we have seen much change. Today, the environment is not as rich as it was before the House on the Water People came. Conflicts between our tribe and the House on the Water People still exist. The harvest and management of fisheries is a contentious issue, despite court decisions affirming our right to half of the fish in our waters and our right to co-manage our resources with federal and state authorities.

Years ago, elders were the primary teachers. In the recent past, official education policies separated children from their families, interrupting the passage of ancestral knowledge. In the 1930s, one of our people gave his land so that we could have public schools on our reservation. Now we have graduated tribal members into the fields of medicine, veterinary science, health, biology, museum studies, education, and law.

But we still fish and teach about the whale hunt. Elders still teach basketry skills, and Makahs are still famous for their fine weaving. The language of our people is spoken by children, and our young people are proud to be Makah.

"My mother had to translate for the Indian

agent. . . . He called her out of school

and told her to explain to her father that

he could only have one wife. He had to choose.

Well, he didn't pick my grandmother,

so she had to move. But we all used to get

together at night sometimes anyway.

Tell stories. Sing."

—Anonymous (Makah), early 1900s

Makah women. Washington State. (N36535)

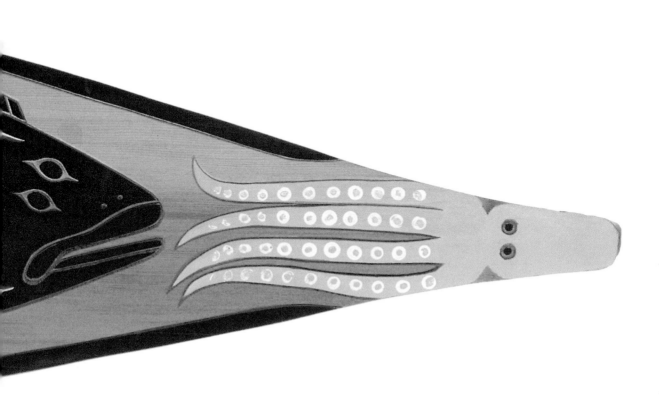

THE HUNTER OF THE WHALE

Our people learned to make a living from the sea, and to respect the power of the ocean and its inhabitants. The whale hunt has been an important part of our lives for a thousand years. Our treaty secured our right to hunt whales, because our negotiators knew that the whale would always be a part of our lives.

By the 1920s, we were no longer hunting whales. The herds had been devastated by commercial whalers. Yet our elders still taught us about whaling. Our social and ceremonial structure still revolves around the whale hunt and living properly so that we deserve the whale's attentions. We continue to discuss whaling with our children. Our families still keep collections of whaling gear.

Wood paddle (and detail) representing fish, bear mask, bear paw, and octopus, by Bill Martin (Makah), 1992. Neah Bay, Washington. (25.3355)

Quechua man in dance mask.
Peru. (N37999)

QUECHUA

The Persistence of the Inka World View

Ramiro Matos (Quechua) and Jorge Flores Ochoa (Quechua)

"O Sun Inka, our father, . . . we beg that your children, the Inka . . . may be conquerors always, for this you have created them . . . ."

—Inka prayer, 1575

Today the term Quechua refers to both language and ethnic identity. The Quechua people, one of many groups native to the region of the Andes Mountains in South America, are the descendants of the Inka. The Inka were the children of the sun.

Inka culture originated in the twelfth century in the southeastern highlands of what is now Peru. From A.D. 1470 until 1532, the Inka rose to power and expanded across western South America over some of the world's most rugged territory. Using a remarkable administrative system, Inka rulers, governing from their capital at Cuzco, forged a single empire, which they called Tawantinsuyu, from a diverse group of conquered tribes, kingdoms, and nations. At its height, their empire spread over a territory more than 5,500 kilometers (3,400 miles) in length.

The Inka empire came to an end in 1532, when Spaniards invaded the region, but the Inka people did not disappear. Despite centuries of colonial rule, during which everything Inka was outlawed, the Inka live on—in the traditions and prayers and lives of the Quechua people.

ORIGINS: MOTHER EARTH, FATHER SUN

The Quechua universe is vast, open, and dual. Nothing is isolated; everything was created in pairs, including mountains, rivers, stones, animals, and spirits. That is why people have two eyes, two hands, two feet. The earth has two halves: an upper and a lower. The earth is also the center that joins and divides sunset and sunrise. The Quechua concept of duality stresses the complementary nature of all things.

Figures such as this are called *torito de Pukara*. On the bull's chest is an abstract symbolic image of the sacred Inka snake, Amaru. This figure, combining the Spanish bull and the Inka snake, is also called *toro encantado*, a mythical figure that lives in a *qocha* (lake) and comes out at night. The toro encantado may carry people off, but this is not considered a bad thing: it means a better life because it represents a return to the qocha.

Right: Ceramic *torito de Pukara* (bull), ca. 1940. Peru. 27.7 x 33 cm. (20.8146) *Opposite:* Quechua flute player. Peru. (N37998)

56

Quechua stories explain that Pachamama (Mother Earth) and Inti (Father Sun) together created the earth and everything that exists on it. Pachamama is the creator and protector of human beings, animals, plants, and things such as textiles, tools, and houses. She gives her life and soul for the welfare of the people, although they do not always reciprocate equally. Inti sends sunlight and rain to fertilize the earth. The sea and lakes are female, and the mountains are male. Rivers are the veins of the earth, and give life to nature.

DEVASTATION: CONQUEST, RESISTANCE, AND SUBVERSION

The Andean region was changed forever after 1532. Spain installed a new system of government. The Inka people and their subjects became a class at the bottom of the social structure. Members of the Inka nobility lost their privileges, Inka socio-political

Q'eros are important symbolic objects among Andean people, especially the Inka. They were made and used in pairs and handed down through generations as heirlooms. During the colonial era, the Spanish banned the making of q'eros with Inka images on them. This q'ero depicts an Andean bullfighter. Unlike Spanish bullfighters, the bullfighter does not use a cape; he uses a lance (rojón) to tease the bull.

Opposite: Wooden q'ero (ritual cup), 17th c. Colonial Peru. Painted wood, height 19.3 cm.; 16.8 cm. diam. (10.5365) *Right:* Aymara silver figure of man with llama, late 18th/early 19th c. Bolivia. Length 7 cm. (22.1900)

organization disappeared, and indigenous Andean communities became isolated from one another as they had been before the Inka empire. Native people were converted, often forcibly, to Catholicism, and churches were constructed on ancient sacred sites with stones taken from Inka ruins. The Inka empire had a population of more than 10,000,000; fifty years after the conquest, fewer than 500,000 remained.

As a result of Spanish prohibitions on traditional art forms and motifs, Native Andean beliefs had to be expressed in subtle and complex ways. To this day, many Inka beliefs survive among the Quechua people. Andean beliefs were incorporated into Christian doctrine: the Virgin Mary was identified with Pachamama, and the Christian God with Inti. Andean Native leaders adopted Spanish strategies and tools: they appropriated horses and guns and led a series of uprisings against Spanish rule.

Wamani

In Tarmatambo, every mountain has a *wamani*. The wamani of this place is named Warangayoj, the same as the mountain. Wamani are the spirits of the hills, some say the gods of them. They are the true owners of the countryside and all that lives and grows there. From the water of the lagoons and streams, to the grass of the meadows, all this belongs to the wamani. Wild animals——the great cats, viscachas, vicuñas, birds, and others——are their property. Birds are their messengers and bring news of their kingdom to the earth, announcing rain, storms, snow, deaths, and misfortunes. The viscacha is the animal of love, happiness, and the hopes of each new day; the vicuña provides wool and meat. To hunt these animals, we ask consent from the Warangayoj-wamani, and offer him payment. Otherwise, the animals remain hidden in the mountains and can never be captured. When the offerings are to the wamani's liking, he not only permits the hunt, but rewards us with tender-meated animals or those recently born, which we can raise for our benefit. Our animals enjoy the grass of these fields. Two times a year we make gifts to the wamani, during the carnivals and during the month of animal rituals.

The water from the Huaylara and Huachacc springs that we use for irrigation in Tarmatambo is a blessing from the Warangayoj-wamani. Some years ago, the authorities forgot to bring his offering, and as a consequence the springs began to dry and there was not enough water for irrigation. Faced with this, the community mobilized to have a party and offer a large payment. Along with the gift, we sacrificed a bull and buried it. The wamani was satisfied and the springs returned. We always have to be on time with that payment.

Inside the hill the wamani has a beautiful house, adorned with gold and silver. Access to this residence is through a sacred cave that no one knows. Sometimes a man can be invited there, but anyone who accepts the invitation and decides to enter the interior is never allowed to return. The wamani prefers to tempt young men and maiden women.

There are two kinds of wamani, one great and the other less so. The most important and powerful one is named Machu-wamani. He is the leader of the others——the *uchuc-wamani*—— and gives them orders. They say that Machu-wamani lives inside the Yarupajá, a mountain covered with snow, in a house of gold built on a large lake. When a uchuc-wamani gets angry, he generally shows it by drying the streams or halting the rain, so that the cattle don't have water to drink or pasture to graze. Machu-wamani never gets angry. When the day comes that he does, there will be a catastrophe on the earth. The ground will tremble and the waters of the lakes will leave their beds, flooding valleys and destroying towns. It will be the end of the world and of humankind. We must hope this misfortune never comes to pass and Machu-wamani always lives happily in his kingdom.

When people have faith in the wamani and bring him offerings regularly, we do not have to wait for his blessings; we feel protected and secure. Many times it seems as if we are accompanied by something other than human. Although the wamani cannot be touched, sometimes we hear his voice in the solitude of the countryside. At some moments in the night he appears in the shape of a man—talking, guiding, and advising. Other times he has presented himself in the form of a bird, announcing rain, storms, and especially solar and lunar eclipses and tremors and earthquakes.

After the conquest by the Spanish, the wamani had terrible fights with the saint Santiago, whom the whites brought to dominate the country. This Catholic saint wanted to snatch the power of the wamani, taking control of the rain, thunder, clouds, and, eventually, the field animals. The two fought for many years, but neither became the victor. Santiago mounted his white horse and made himself ruler of the clouds and the thunder, while the wamani still possess the mountains and the living things of the earth. We have a picture of Santiago in our homes. We celebrate his day every July 25. At the same time, we prepare an offering for the wamani, which we bring to him in the night. The saint Santiago is worshipped in the Catholic church and the offering to the wamani is delivered to a sacred place that only the *auqui* (spiritual leaders) know.

The elders say that wamani like pretty women. Tarmatambo has never heard news of a wamani with a woman we know. However, there was a case in Cajas in which a woman had a relationship with a wamani and became pregnant. The child came into the world talking. He spoke with the spirit and saw things that people could never see, but he soon died and was taken by his father to the kingdom of the wamani. The mother remains sad and alone. Men look at her with fear and respect, and although they come to help her plant and harvest her crops, no one has ever tried to fall in love with her. This woman has never married any man but always receives all their attention. She has the best crop and the best cattle of the community, and for this reason she lives comfortably.

— *Pablo Huamán (Quechua),*
Agustín Melendez (Quechua),
and Teodoro Ollero (Quechua), 1996

SURVIVAL: THE PERSISTENCE OF INKA

Although Inka culture was banned during centuries of Spanish colonial rule, much of it survives in the persistence and vitality of Quechua traditions—in offerings that honor Pachamama, in veneration of ancient *huacas* (sacred places), in traditional agricultural seasonal celebrations and rituals, and in the Andean folk drama called Ollantay.

Ollantay, named after a town in the Sacred Valley near Cuzco, is a form of oral history. At the end of the 1600s, actors began to perform dramas that brought to life Inka stories about the origin and history of the Andean world. These dramas use Andean dancing and music, combined with Christian symbols. To the Quechua, the plays are not re-enactments, but real events. They are not the work of a single author or composer, but the creation of the whole community. The Spaniards considered Ollantay to be a form of rebellion and banned the dramas, but the Quechua performed them clandestinely and still perform them today.

Objects from Inka, colonial, and modern times show how certain powerful and sacred institutions have persisted and changed in the Andean universe during the last 450 years: Pachamama, Inti, and *wamani*, the mountain spirits, survive, and so does the idea of Inka as a sacred entity and the midpoint in a dual universe.

Quechua officials. Peru.

(N37997)

The term Inka has many differ-

ent meanings: the Sapa Inka

was the emperor, who ruled as

the son of Inti. He was a sacred

and divine person sent to gov-

ern the people on earth. Inka is

also the government and the

state. Inka is that which is infi-

nite and ancient.

Inka also means the center of

the earth, and the midpoint

Quechua merchants selling
ponchos, 1924. Huancayo,
Peru. Photo by A.H. Verrill.
(N10153)

between the earth and the sun.

Sunset is called "the moment of

Inka." When two groups meet

in a celebration, they say:

"Inkaicusunchik"—"We will make

Inka." To people from the

Cuzco area, Inka today means

something ancient and

spiritually powerful—a strong,

deep feeling.

— *Ramiro Matos (Quechua)*

WESTERN APACHE

Resistance and Renewal

Dale Curtis Miles (San Carlos Apache)

We call ourselves N'de, the People. We are the Western Apache, one of the six major divisions of the Apache people of the Southwest, related culturally and linguistically to the Chiricahua, Jicarilla, Mescalero, Lipan, and Kiowa Apache. Also related to this group are the Navajo. The languages and dialects of these peoples are part of the Southern Athapaskan language family. In turn, Southern Athapaskans are related to the Northern Athapaskans of Canada and Alaska.

We were never one united tribe but rather organize ourselves as sub-tribes that are further divided into bands and then into local family units or clusters. Our elaborate clan system extends through all the Western Apache country. Clan—traced through a person's mother—is considered a blood relationship, so a person can claim a connection to a band a hundred miles away.

Ceremonies that are important to the people all have their origins in the stories of the people. We do not like our stories referred to as myths; our sense of who we are and our world view are wrapped up in these stories. Even clothing, tools, baskets, and other material culture so important in everyday life have direct links to the stories of the people.

White Mountain Apache man,
1907. Photo by Fred Harvey.

(T6080)

Above: San Carlos Apache
female doll, ca. 1880.
Arizona. Cotton and yarn,
height 39.5 cm. (8.5592)
Right: Apache burden basket,
ca. 1910. Arizona. Height
39.5 cm. (8.9926)

SURVIVAL: ADAPTING TO A CHANGING ENVIRONMENT

It is ironic that officers and soldiers in the U.S. military, while contributing mightily
to the demise of much of the traditional Apache lifeways, were also some of the first
tourists, buying Apache-made souvenirs in the Southwest. A part of our culture might
have disappeared if not for these Anglo collectors and traders.

Throughout this century, we have fought to overcome the legacy of the early
reservation years, gaining new understanding and confidence in dealing with the
government to preserve our rights. We are striving to become economically
self-sufficient, and through adaptation, resistance, and struggle, Apache religion,
language, and culture have survived.

I have a picture of my mother's mother, taken around 1900, dressed like this. Camp dresses are still a common sight around San Carlos, though women today wear a "contemporary style," which has a shorter and less full skirt. My wife wears this style all the time. My mother is a dressmaker, and she specializes in it. Even though people call this style contemporary, it was also worn in the olden days.

—*Dale Curtis Miles*
(San Carlos Apache)

69

White Mountain Apache woman, 1919. Arizona. Photo by E. H. Davis. (P2198)

In Apache tradition, owls are associated with ghosts.

70

The man I heard singing most at victory dances was a little short man called Hastin Diłhił (Old Man Black). He used to wear an owl-feather cap. He knew those songs the best. But I don't know who made the songs in the beginning. They came down from the beginning of the Earth I guess. I think he didn't make any of these himself, but learned them at the dances when he was a boy. I wanted to know where these songs came from so I asked my mother's mother one time, "Is this your song?" "No, I did not make these. They come from long, long ago," she said. No one ever taught a man these songs. He just picked them up at dances. He never paid to learn them.

The little old man who used to sing at victory dances didn't get paid. But he was given a piece of meat. He was old and used a cane to get about with.

One time we asked the old man, "Why do you wear that owl cap on your head?" "Well, when you walk alone at night and wear it, nothing bothers you. You can't hear any owls at all," he said.

—*Anonymous (Western Apache), 1930s*

TRADITIONAL LIFEWAYS

In the beginning, Usen the Creator sent Ga'an to guide the people. He taught the people how to walk in the Holy Life Way (Enzu). The people were taught to be kind to each other, especially to those who had less, to be respectful in hunting and warfare, and to live in harmony with each other and the land.

In contrast to popular misconceptions created and maintained by newcomers to our region, Apaches were not warlike. Our traditional lifeways allowed us to move with the seasons to gather and hunt the necessities that kept us clothed, fed, sheltered, and happy. We raided for food only during times of extreme shortage. Wars were not randomly fought, but were well-planned campaigns to avenge injustices against our people.

The gun and the horse expanded the range, effectiveness, and reputation of our warriors. The horse, introduced by the Spanish in the 1600s, became an integral part of our traditional life. Later we would learn to use guns gathered through trade, raids, or war.

CONFINEMENT AND CHANGING LIFEWAYS

The arrival of outside settlers to our region brought hostilities and change. Settlers had little regard for our ties to the land. Our grandfathers and great-grandfathers fought to protect our traditions and culture, but, overwhelmed by superior numbers and modern technology, our people were forced to give up our life of the wind.

In 1872 the San Carlos Indian Agency was established by the U.S. Army and government, and thousands of Western Apaches and other tribal groups—many our traditional enemies—were forced to live there together. Under this oppressive system, our culture changed rapidly. Many ceremonies and customs were discouraged or forbidden outright. We were known by identification numbers instead of names. Cut off from our traditions, we starved physically, emotionally, and spiritually.

Opposite: "Josh, Chief, San Carlos Apaches," 1898. Photo by F.A. Rinehart. (N19290A)

CHANGING WOMAN

The most important ceremony of Western Apache is the Nah-ih-es', or Sunrise Dance, as it is called today. To us, the Nah-ih-es'—which is also known as the Changing Woman Ceremony and was once given to every young girl as she began the transformation to womanhood—is not just an individual rite of passage but a confirmation of our survival. The origins of all that is good in life are part of the ceremony, in which Changing Woman provides blessings to all Apaches through songs and prayer.

74

The Apache ideal is to look as much like Changing Woman as possible, so from her elaborately beaded moccasins to the white abalone shell on her head, the young girl becomes the person-ification of Changing Woman.

The four-day ceremony requires great commitment and endurance on the part of the girl, her family, and her extended family, and distant clan relatives may be called upon to assist in funding this community event.

There was a time when Changing Woman lived all alone. Longing for children, she slept with the Sun and not long after gave birth to Slayer of Monsters. Four days later, Changing Woman became pregnant by water and gave birth to Born of Water. As Slayer of Monsters and Born of Water grew up, Changing Woman taught them how to live, and after they left home, following what she had taught them, they rid the earth of most of its evil. When Changing Woman reached old age, she walked toward the east. After a while, she saw herself coming toward herself, and when she came together, there was only one, the young one. Then she was like a young girl all over again.

In this way, Changing Woman offers a young girl long life, and the abilities of someone always young.

Western (San Carlos?) Apache
woman, ca. 1884. Photo by
A.F. Randall. (P6813)

Goyathlay (Geronimo),
far right, Chiricahua Apache
tribal leader, his son, and two
men. (P13279)

CONTRIBUTORS

Greig Arnold is a carver and Founding Director of the Makah Cultural and Research Center.

Charlotte Heth is an ethnomusicologist and Assistant Director for Public Programs at the National Museum of the American Indian.

Richard W. Hill, Sr. is Assistant Professor of American Studies at SUNY/Buffalo and former Special Assistant to the Director of the National Museum of the American Indian. He lives in Sanborn, New York, on the Tuscarora Reservation.

George P. Horse Capture is Deputy Assistant Director for Cultural Resources at the National Museum of the American Indian, New York City. His home is at Fort Belknap, Montana.

Ramiro Matos, Professor Emeritus of Archaeology at the University of San Marcos in Lima, Peru, is Cultural Specialist for Central and South America at the National Museum of the American Indian.

Dale Curtis Miles is Tribal Historian of the San Carlos Apache.

Jorge Flores Ochoa is a member of the Faculty of Social Sciences of the National University of San Antonio Abad in Cuzco, Peru.

W. Richard West has been Director of the National Museum of the American Indian for the past six years. An attorney, he has devoted much of his professional and personal life to working with American Indians on cultural, educational, legal, and governmental issues.

SOURCES

FOREWORD

"...and for each line that was spoken, ..."
Keith Basso, editor, *Western Apache Raiding and Warfare*, from the notes of
Grenville Gordon (Tucson: University of Arizona, 1966): 29.

Her Eyes Grey, whose English name was Anna Price, was born about 1835.
She was the oldest daughter of Diablo, an important White Mountain
Apache chief.

NORTHERN PLAINS

"They brought us here ..."
"Condition of the Indian Tribes," *Senate Report 156, 39th Congress, 2nd Session*
(Washington, D.C.: Government Printing Office, 1867).

Dream of the Crow and Owl
Frances Densmore, *Teton Sioux Music*, Bureau of American Ethnology
Bulletin 61 (Washington, D.C.: Government Printing Office, 1918):
184–88.

Śiya'ka (Teal Duck), who was also known as Wanbli'wana'peya (Eagle Who
Frightens), was the elected chief of a band of Yankton Nakota. He was born
about 1840 and described this dream, shortly before he died in 1913, to an
ethnomusicologist visiting the Standing Rock Reservation in the Dakotas.

TUSCARORA

The Young Girl and the Thunderbeings
Adapted from Iroquoian cosmology collected by Tuscarora museologist and
ethnologist J.N.B. Hewitt, published in *21st Annual Report of the Bureau of
American Ethnology, 1899–1900* (Washington, D.C.: Government Printing
Office, 1903): 127–339; and *43rd Annual Report of the Bureau of American
Ethnology, 1925–26* (Washington, D.C.: Government Printing Office,
1928): 449–819.

CHEROKEE

"...In History, little is said ..." and *"A Witness Remembers the Removal"*
Wahnenauhi (Lucy Lowery Hoyt Keys), "The Wahnenauhi Manuscript:
Historical Sketches of the Cherokees Together with Some of Their Customs,
Traditions, and Superstitions," edited by Jack Frederick Kilpatrick, *Bureau of
American Ethnology Bulletin 196* (Washington, D.C.: Government Printing
Office, 1966): 175, 206–207.

Wahnenauhi, Mrs. Lucy Lowery Hoyt Keys, was born in 1831 into a promi-
nent family of planters and missionaries and graduated from the Cherokee
Female Seminary in 1855, a member of the school's first graduating classes.
She died in 1912 in Pleasant Hill, near Vinita, Oklahoma.

The Ball Game of the Birds and Animals and *The Pheasant Beating Corn*
James Mooney, "Myths of the Cherokee," *19th Annual Report of the Bureau of
American Ethnology, 1897–98* (Washington, D.C.: Government Printing
Office, 1900): 286–87, 290.

A'yûñ'inĭ, also called Swimmer, was born about 1835, just before the
Removal. He was tutored as a child to be a keeper of the traditions, religious
leader, and doctor, and did not speak English. During his life, he made a
written record of stories, songs, and sacred knowledge in the Cherokee
alphabet. A'yûñ'inĭ died in 1899.

Itāgûñ'nähĭ, whose English name was John Ax, was born about 1800 and
remembered such events as the Cherokees' war with the Creeks in 1812.
He was not formally trained in the traditions, but learned them as a boy
attending the *âs*, the Cherokee sweat lodge. He died in about 1900.

MAKAH

"My mother had to translate ..."
Ruth Kirk, *Tradition and Change on the Northwest Coast* (University of
Washington Press, 1986): 228.

"You, Born to Be Given ..."
Franz Boas, quoted by Kirk, *Tradition and Change on the Northwest Coast*
(1986): 126.

"They used to burn them . . ."
Kirk, *Tradition and Change on the Northwest Coast* (1986): 223.

Deer and the Canary Bird Dancers
Frances Densmore, "Nootka and Quileute Music," *Smithsonian Institution Bureau of American Ethnology Bulletin 124* (Washington, D.C.: Government Printing Office, 1939): 208.

Mrs. Wilson Parker was raised in the traditional Makah way of life. She did not speak English, and her daughter, Hazel Parker Butler, served as translator of her stories. Mrs. Parker died sometime between 1926, the latest possible date when this story might have been collected, and 1939, the year it was published.

QUECHUA

"O Sun Inka, our father . . ."
Cristobal de Molina (el Cusqueño), "*Relacion de las fabulas i ritos de los Ingas* [ca. 1575]. In "*Fabulas y mitos de los incas,*" edited by Henrique Urbano and Pierre Duviols, *Cronicas de America* series (Madrid: Historia 16, 1989): 47–134.

Wamani
Ramiro Matos, field notes, 1996 (unpublished). Pablo Huamán (born 1926), Agustín Melendez (born 1931), and Teodoro Ollero (born 1928) live in the Tarmatambo region of Peru.

WESTERN APACHE

Changing Woman
Thomas E. Mails, *The People Called Apache.* (New York: Prentice-Hall, 1974): 76.

How One Man Lived to an Old Age
Keith Basso, editor, *Western Apache Raiding and Warfare* (1966): 282–83.
The anonymous Western Apache man who told the story of the owl-feather cap was himself quite old when he was interviewed in the early 1930s.

PHOTO CREDITS

The objects in this book were photographed by Pam Dewey, Janine Jones, and Katherine Fogden of the Office of Photo Services of the National Museum of the American Indian. Historical images are from the NMAI Photo Archives, except where noted.

All images © Smithsonian Institution, except where noted.